Date: 6/29/18

J 946 MAR
Markovics, Joyce L.,
Spain /

Spain

by Joyce Markovics

Consultant: Marjorie Faulstich Orellana, PhD
Professor of Urban Schooling
University of California, Los Angeles

BEARPORT
PUBLISHING

New York, New York

Credits

Cover, © Marcos Mesa Sam Wordley/Shutterstock and © dimbar76/Shutterstock; TOC, © Miramiska/ Shutterstock; 4, © TeodorStefanov/iStock; 5T, © Tono Balaguer/AGE Fotostock; 5B, © atikinka/ Shutterstock; 7, © LucVi/Shutterstock; 8, © nito/Shutterstock; 9, © Migel/Shutterstock; 10BL, © Gonzalo Azumendi/AGE fotostock/Alamy Photo Stock; 10–11, © EHStock/iStock; 11BR, © Artur Bogacki/ Dreamstime; 12, © Everett Historical/Shutterstock; 13T, © KarSol/Shutterstock; 13B, © Marques/ Shutterstock; 14–15, © Iakov Filimonov/Shutterstock; 15BL, © nito100/iStock; 16BL, © Vladitto/ Shutterstock; 16–17, © Valery Egorov/Shutterstock; 18, © Caron Badkin/Shutterstock; 19, © holbox/ Shutterstock; 20, © stockcreations/Shutterstock; 21, © Foodpictures/Shutterstock; 22–23, © Marcin Krzyzak/Shutterstock; 24, © Maxisport/Shutterstock; 25, © Sergei Bachlakov/ Dreamstime; 26–27, © Silvia B. Jakiello/Shutterstock; 27TR, © Brian Maudsley/Shutterstock; 28, © Mmeeds/Dreamstime; 29, © SUSANA VERA/REUTERS/Newscom; 30T, © Viktor Kunz/ Shutterstock and © spinetta/Shutterstock; 30B, © HEINO KALIS/REUTERS/Alamy Photo Stock; 31 (T to B), © dimbar76/Shutterstock, © Everett Historical/Shutterstock, © Luis Cagiao/ Shutterstock, © costas anton dumitrescu/Shutterstock, © Israel Hervas Bengochea/Shutterstock, and © g-stockstudio/iStock; 32, © Vitaly Raduntsev/Shutterstock.

Publisher: Kenn Goin
Senior Editor: Joyce Tavolacci
Creative Director: Spencer Brinker
Design: Debrah Kaiser
Photo Researcher: Thomas Persano

Library of Congress Cataloging-in-Publication Data

Names: Markovics, Joyce L., author.
Title: Spain / by Joyce Markovics.
Description: New York, New York : Bearport Publishing, 2018. | Series: Countries we come from | Audience: Ages 5 to 8. | Includes bibliographical references and index.
Identifiers: LCCN 2017007490 (print) | LCCN 2017011317 (ebook) | ISBN 9781684022519 (library bound) | ISBN 9781684023059 (Ebook)
Subjects: LCSH: Spain—Juvenile literature.
Classification: LCC DP17 .M295 2018 (print) | LCC DP17 (ebook) | DDC 946—dc23
LC record available at https://lccn.loc.gov/2017007490

For more information, write to Bearport Publishing Company, Inc., 45 West 21st Street, Suite 3B, New York, New York 10010. Printed in the United States of America.

10 9 8 7 6 5 4 3 2 1

Contents

Striking

Colorful

Welcoming

Spain is a big country in southwestern Europe.

It's located on a peninsula (puh-NIN-suh-luh).

Water surrounds the country on three sides.

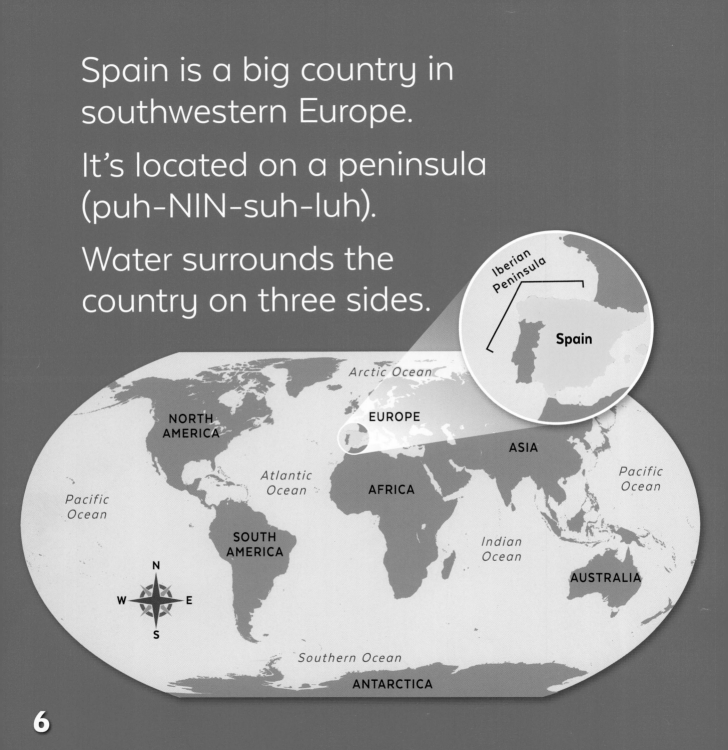

Iberian Peninsula

Spain

Arctic Ocean

NORTH AMERICA

EUROPE

ASIA

Atlantic Ocean

AFRICA

Pacific Ocean

Pacific Ocean

SOUTH AMERICA

Indian Ocean

AUSTRALIA

N
W   E
S

Southern Ocean

ANTARCTICA

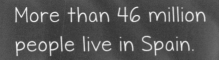

More than 46 million people live in Spain.

The landscape of Spain is varied and beautiful.

There are sandy beaches and soaring mountains.

The central part of the country is a huge, flat **plateau**.

Farmers raise horses and cows on the plateau.

9

People have been living in Spain for thousands of years.

During that time, different groups controlled the land.

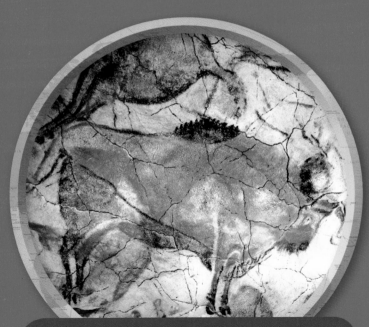

This cave drawing in Spain was created about 18,000 years ago.

They included the Romans, the Visigoths, and the Moors.

Córdoba **Mosque** was built by the Moors in the year 780.

In the 1930s, a **civil war** broke out in Spain.

A cruel man named Francisco Franco became ruler.

The Spanish Civil War lasted from 1936 to 1939.

After Franco died in 1975, Spain became a free country.

Francisco Franco

A memorial to Spain's dead soldiers

More than 500,000 people lost their lives during the war.

Spain has many large cities.

The **capital** is Madrid.

It's also the biggest city in the country.

More than three million people live there.

Barcelona is Spain's second-largest city.

Spain's cities are filled with amazing buildings.

The church of Sagrada Família is one of them.

It's been under construction for more than 100 years!

16

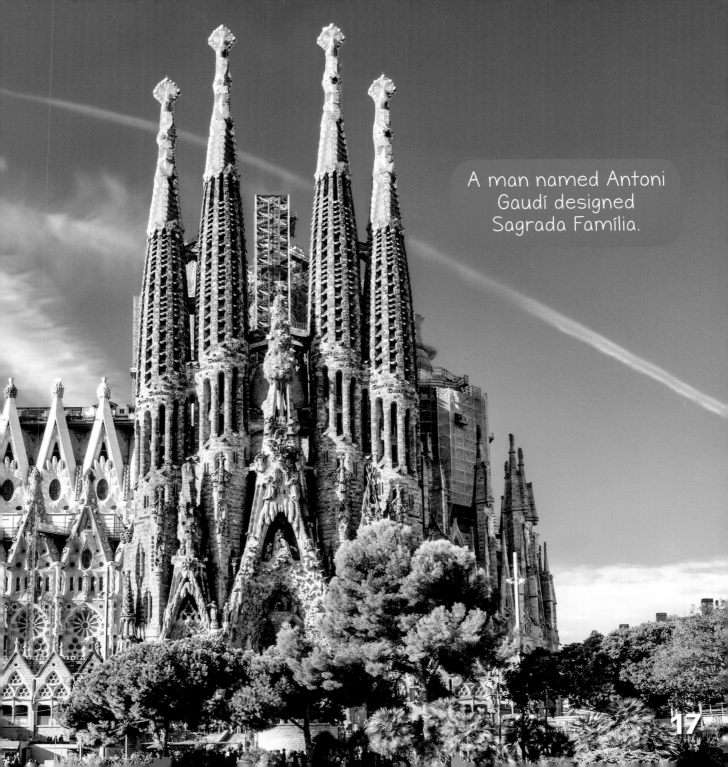

A man named Antoni Gaudí designed Sagrada Família.

The main language in Spain is Spanish.

This is how you say *the sun*:

El sol (el SOHL)

This is how you say *beautiful*:

Hermosa
(hehr-MOH-sah)

The Basque and Catalan languages are also spoken in Spain.

Spanish food is famous worldwide.

A favorite dish is called paella (pah-YEH-uh).

Rice, seafood, and spices are simmered together.

Tapas (TAH-puhs) are tasty snacks.

They are served cold and hot.

Tapas include small plates of olives, ham, and cheese.

Musicians **strum** guitars.

A dancer swings her arms and stamps her feet.

The group is performing flamenco.

It's a well-known style of music and dance in Spain.

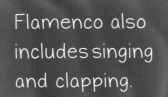

Flamenco also includes singing and clapping.

What's the most popular sport in Spain?

Soccer!

Spanish players are some of the best in the world.

Fans cheer for their team.

Soccer is called *fútbol* (FOOT-bole) in Spain.

Thousands of **festivals** are held in Spain.

During Las Fallas in València, people party in the streets.

They make huge paper sculptures.

The paper sculptures can be more than 30 feet (9 m) tall.

At the end of the festival, the sculptures are burned!

A rocket launches into the sky in the city of Pamplona.

It's the start of the San Fermín festival.

The San Fermín festival is held in July.

Bulls thunder through the streets. People run to escape them!

Fast Facts

Capital city: Madrid

Population of Spain: More than 46 million

Main language: Spanish

Money: Euro

Major religion: Roman Catholic

Neighboring countries: Portugal and France

Cool Fact: At a festival in Buñol, Spain, people throw ripe tomatoes at each other!

Glossary

capital (KAP-uh-tuhl) a city where a country's government is based

civil war (SIV-il WOR) a war between groups of people within the same country

festivals (FES-tuh-vuhls) celebrations

mosque (MOSK) a building used for worship by Muslim people

plateau (pla-TOH) an area of high, flat land

strum (STRUHM) to play a guitar by running one's fingers lightly across the strings

Index

Read More

Grack, Rachel. *Spain (Blastoff! Readers: Exploring Countries).* New York: Scholastic (2010).

Guillain, Charlotte. *Spain (Countries Around the World).* Portsmouth, NH: Heinemann (2012).

Learn More Online

To learn more about Spain, visit
www.bearportpublishing.com/CountriesWeComeFrom

About the Author

Joyce Markovics lives in a very old house along the Hudson River. She hasn't yet visited Spain but would love to take in its splendors.